Cerebration

Rob Chaseman

BALBOA.PRESS
A DIVISION OF HAY HOUSE

Balboa Press books may be ordered through booksellers or by contacting:

Balboa Press
A Division of Hay House
1663 Liberty Drive
Bloomington, IN 47403
www.balboapress.com
844-682-1282

Print information available on the last page.

ISBN: 979-8-7652-4124-0 (sc)
ISBN: 979-8-7652-4125-7 (e)

Balboa Press rev. date: 05/27/2023

Cerebration*

1. *n.* any kind of conscious thinking, such as pondering or problem solving[1]

2. *n.* the act of thinking; consideration; thought[2]

3. **n.* thinking about my own 'stupid little wisdoms'

---

[1] American Psychological Association (n.d.) In American Psychological Association Dictionary of Psychology. Retrieved May 26, 2023, from https://dictionary.apa.org/cerebration

[2] Dictionary.com (n.d.) In Dictionary.com. Retrieved May 26, 2023, from https://dictionary.com/browse/cerebration

Acknowledgements

Thank you to Brett, Christine, Kerry, Matt, Marie, Jason, and Joanne for their assistance with this publication.

Preface

This book is a compilation of some thoughts that have helped me navigate a life sometimes filled with struggle. A life I am grateful for. My hope is that one or more of these thoughts may bring others the meaning, fulfillment, and understanding that they have brought me.

Introduction

We may be like flowers.

Every rose is different from every daisy. Every orchid is different from every dandelion. No two roses, daisies, orchids, dandelions, or any other flowers are alike. When we celebrate the uniqueness of each flower, we may be able to revere the shared beauty in them all.

Thought 1

When we don't judge, but rather examine our thoughts, feelings, and perceptions, we may diminish dissonance within ourselves and better understand our world and our place in it.

Thought 2

Sometimes we may become accustomed to our lives being filled with the burden of having struggles. We may find comfort in the discomfort of struggling because the burden is so familiar. Our struggles may not be a burden, but rather a desirable choice. When we welcome a struggle that is congruent with our aspirations, it may be easier, more comfortable and familiar, and even inspiring to struggle toward our goals.

Thought 3

It may be difficult to accept that where we are may be just where we need to be.

Thought 4

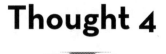

A perceived weakness may become an acquired strength.

Thought 5

Knowledge may be the best way of defining something in order to understand it, until a better explanation is discovered.

Thought 6

Some discomforting feelings that are difficult to experience, may be valuable to experience.

Thought 7

We may all have passionate ideas, concepts and beliefs about the same subjects. Disagreements may be natural. They may all be valid, deserve respect, and may be debated healthily.

Thought 8

Sometimes we may only accept the love of others in the capacity in which we love ourselves.

Thought 9

Even when anger is justified, expressing it towards ourselves or others may be harmful.

Thought 10

Some thoughts may not be worth thinking about.

Thought 11

Concepts, theories, and beliefs may not be truths. They may be frameworks that we use to help us navigate through life.

Thought 12

When there may be multiple interpretations of what something means, no one may be right or wrong for having conflicting ideas or beliefs. We may find it useful to understand alternative perspectives.

Thought 13

Change may often involve discomfort. In order to achieve desired change, it may be necessary to tolerate an acceptable amount of feeling uncomfortable.

Thought 14

We may increase awareness when we integrate knowledge emotionally rather than just knowing it rationally.

Thought 15

Something good for us may often feel uncomfortable, awkward, scary or incongruent because it may be novel and unknown. The more we experience this, what is novel at first, may have the capacity to become known and even understood. Eventually, what we truly know and understand as being good for us may lead to feelings of contentment and joy.

Thought 16

Having a goal of striving for an outcome may be better than having the expectation of reaching that outcome. Expectations of attaining outcomes may lead to disappointment because our only barometer of success may be achieving that outcome. The goal of working towards a desired outcome may give us the ability to appreciate our efforts and progress along the way, which may be a better measurement of our successes and achievement.

Thought 17

When we don't judge where we are, or where we have been, we may be able to concentrate on where we are going.

Thought 18

Mistakes may not be flaws. They may be natural everyday occurrences to learn and grow from.

Thought 19

When we ruminate about, judge, or don't accept our past, we may become stuck in it. If we accept the past, we may be able to apply its lessons towards our present and future.

Thought 20

Sometimes what we need and what we want may be two different things.

Thought 21

When we pay attention to our thoughts, feelings, perceptions, and actions in the present moment, a more intimate connection with our experience may develop.

Thought 22

Recalling fond memories and looking forward to things may have the ability to make us feel good about ourselves.

Thought 23

Applying any sort of description of ourselves to ourselves may not be entirely accurate. All of our qualities may be subjective, and may be of a transient nature. To label ourselves may sometimes inhibit our growth, especially if those labels do not incorporate the ability to change.

Thought 24

To be vulnerable may be a strength. It may be a risk worth taking. Even when the outcome is not favorable, it may have a worthwhile lesson.

Thought 25

Trusting may come with many fears. With repeated experience taking the risk to trust, we may learn how to better navigate the process of trusting. This may increase the opportunities for fulfillment and decrease feelings of disappointment.

Thought 26

Achieving something may be fulfilling. It may take multiple attempts to achieve our goals. Without trying, we may lose all opportunity to achieve anything.

Thought 27

When we have faith, we may have hope, no matter what we believe.

Thought 28

Just because we think of something, and are able to do it, may not mean we should.

Thought 29

Since change may be a constant, adaptability and flexibility may be more beneficial than rigidity.

Thought 30

It may be more fulfilling to be interested in the qualities of others, rather than displaying our own qualities.

Thought 31

Teaching and learning may not have to be sequential. They may go hand in hand.

Thought 32

We may learn from our own, and anyone else's attributes and shortcomings.

Thought 33

Sometimes, there may be nothing wrong with being a loser within competition. It may be valuable when we're striving to improve, and may prepare us for natural outcomes in life.

Thought 34

We may need to experience adversity in order to become resilient.

Thought 35

It may create distress to invest in thoughts that exacerbate discomforting emotions. When we understand how and why these thoughts affect our feelings, we may learn how to mitigate our thoughts.

Thought 36

If we are truly tolerant, we may have to be tolerant of those who are intolerant.

Thought 37

Being honest with ourselves may mean paying attention to our unique beliefs, hopes, and aspirations.

Thought 38

Without defining our beliefs from both acquired knowledge and experiential insight, our beliefs may be just as distorted as opinions.

Thought 39

By questioning an idea, concept, or belief that we agree with, we may become more objective.

Thought 40

Without considering the qualities of the source of information, we may not fully discern the accuracy of that information.

Thought 41

By making comparisons with others, we may feel incongruent with ourselves. We may lose the ability to appreciate our own value because we may put more value in others' relative experiences. We may end up dismissing our own unique experience, perspective, qualities, and achievements.

Thought 42

Our perceptions about ourselves may sometimes be skewed and inaccurate. They may often feel like truths. If we believe them, we may make distorted assumptions about ourselves that may lead to confusion, misinterpretation, unhelpful conclusions or discomforting feelings about ourselves.

Thought 43

We may feel love, but have difficulty expressing it. We may also be loved, and have difficulty feeling it.

Thought 44

It may be important to express our love towards others while we are feeling it. It may mean a lot to them as well as ourselves. We may never get that chance again.

Thought 45

Sometimes it may be easier to harbor ill feelings than to forgive. Ill feelings may sometimes deteriorate our sensibilities, while forgiveness may heal, nurture, and restore our capacity to love.

Thought 46

By accepting what we don't know, we may understand more.

Thought 47

We may feel congruent and fulfilled when we understand how to be accountable to others and ourselves.

Thought 48

We may feel more content by knowing when to work, when to rest, when to take care of ourselves, when to take care of others, when to find fulfillment, when to find meaning, when to love, and when to be loved.

Thought 49

Empathy may be a skill that is an ability to understand another's experience. If we have that skill, we may choose to use it compassionately, harmfully, or in some other capacity.

Thought 50

We all may accept and express love in our own individual ways. When we are aware of the ways we express and accept love, we may be able to synchronize with one another, so our love will be truly felt.

Thought 51

Understanding ourselves and others may work best when we concentrate on the qualities that we all share, and celebrate the uniqueness of our individual differences. It may be divisive when we frame our understanding only in terms of how we are different, or in that which separates us.

Thought 52

We may experience what is happening and create an unrealistic positive outlook that may have distorted expectations. When we have a realistic positive outlook about our experience, we may have a more accurate perspective and feel more empowered.

Thought 53

When we use our mental, physical, and emotional resources for the benefit of ourselves or others, we may feel fulfilled. If we don't know how to replenish our resources, or how to use them effectively for ourselves, we may become depleted, and not have any resources for anyone.

Thought 54

Sometimes work may be unfulfilling and have little meaning. Sometimes work may be fulfilling and meaningful. Anytime we work we may need to be rejuvenated.

Thought 55

A distraction may be useful in the moment to escape something, but may often be temporary, and not a solution. When the distraction ends, what we escaped may return in the same capacity. When we incorporate something fulfilling and meaningful, it may diminish or transform what we are escaping.

Thought 56

Sometimes others may love us and want the best for us. They may not have the capacity to express this or support us in a way that is helpful. It may even be harmful, especially when they are fearful or anxious about our welfare.

Thought 57

When we believe ourselves or others to be fragile, there may be an assumption that we are not adequate, competent, or accomplished.

Thought 58

Humor may be enlightening when it creates meaning and new perspectives. When the meaning and new perspectives are at the expense of others it may be harmful.

Thought 59

Being brave may mean doing something while we are afraid.

Thought 60

Choosing to be involved in something easy and enjoyable now may give us immediate satisfaction. We may achieve longer lasting and greater fulfillment by choosing to do something that is harder and uncomfortable in the present that is a step towards our greater aspirations in the future.

Thought 61

Being committed may mean staying dedicated no matter what.

Thought 62

Labeling something as right or wrong, or bad or good, or with any other two polarities, may create an inaccurate conclusion, rather than considering all the various complexities of what we may be labeling.

Thought 63

Labeling ourselves may be empowering when we gain knowledge, insight, and motivation. Labels may also hold us back significantly when we stigmatize, judge, and shame ourselves.

Thought 64

When we label ourselves as having certain characteristics, it may make it difficult to perceive ourselves as anything different, which may inhibit growth and change.

Thought 65

Stigma is a cycle that may be hard to break. The cycle may continue because we may not want to be authentic for fear of being judged, or we may continue to judge others because we may not understand their authentic selves.

Thought 66

If we are stigmatized, we may choose to be our authentic selves all the time, which may lead to judgment and consequences from others, or we may be our true authentic self when the possibility of judgment and consequences have diminished. The latter may eventually create some misunderstanding, because our authentic qualities may seem novel to others. The former may feel more congruent in the present, but may be more difficult to endure.

Thought 67

If fear is at the root of any of our perspectives, we may live in a way to try to alleviate that fear. This may create relief and comfort, but may not be as peaceful as living without the fear.

Thought 68

Fear may be healthy when there is a perceived threat, because we may become necessarily hypervigilant. But if the perceived threat is unrealistic or irrational, fear may be debilitating.

Thought 69

A relationship may be more fulfilling when we share equal reciprocity in the responsibilities of maintaining and fostering the connection.

Thought 70

Sometimes we may be viewed and treated by others based on a distorted perception of who we are, who we have been, or who others want us to be. It may be necessary to advocate for ourselves so others may understand us from our current perspective.

Thought 71

It may increase our understanding when we don't accept an assumption about another as a truth, but rather investigate and clarify our perspective.

Thought 72

The same words or ideas may have different meanings for every person. When we understand the unique meaning others attribute, rather than attributing our own meaning, we may understand others better.

Thought 73

In order to be truly grateful, we may need to appreciate ourselves.

Thought 74

Some questions may have no answer.

Thought 75

When we approach a disagreement with curiosity
we may sharpen our perspective.

Thought 76

Others' ideas, concepts, or insights may be better understood when they are explained through their perspective rather than from our own.

Thought 77

Most anything may fall somewhere on a bell curve of what exists. Everything on the bell curve may be valid, even when it is an outlier.

Thought 78

Others may want us to treat them how they want to be treated, not how we want to be treated.

Thought 79

Nurturing that allows room for failure may empower others, so they may learn from their own mistakes, explore their own solutions, gain their own insight, and become resilient.

Thought 80

Others may have perceptions and perspectives about us which may not be congruent with our own perceptions and perspectives about ourselves. When we understand others' mistaken assumptions, we may have the opportunity to advocate for ourselves.

Thought 81

When we fight for what we believe in rather than against what we disagree with, we may feel more empowered.

Thought 82

When fear and pessimism are predominant, having hope may be empowering.

Thought 83

When we rely on only hoping for the best, we may not be prepared for the worst.

Thought 84

Conflicts and misunderstandings may arise when we may not understand what lens we are perceiving things through, and what lenses others may use.

Thought 85

To love someone may mean to nurture them so they flourish with or without us.

Thought 86

An interpersonal conflict may have little to do with the specific content within an interaction, but rather the underlying miscommunication of our feelings.

Thought 87

Love may be best expressed through care, affection, trust, respect, commitment, honesty, validation, and compassionate empathy.

Thought 88

Conflicts may never be mitigated when we are reactive, defensive, and inserting blame. When we have a curiosity to understand one another, we may mitigate conflicts with kindness, respect, and compassionate empathy.

Thought 89

We may never be ready for what we want to do or be.

Thought 90

A sense of humor may be individualistic. Something funny to us may be hurtful to another.

Thought 91

When we attribute meaning to something ambiguous, we may create unnecessary feelings within ourselves that correlate to the meaning that we attribute.

Thought 92

If our past sentiment and behavior has not been congruent, others may only trust that our intentions are true when our present words are consistent with our actions.

Thought 93

Judging ourselves or others on the past may be a barrier to noticing how we have changed, or how we are in the process of changing.

Thought 94

Others may understand us better when we convey how we feel along with what we think.

Thought 95

Forgiving ourselves may enable us to love and appreciate ourselves more completely.

Thought 96

It may be difficult to communicate effectively when we are emotional, because others may respond to our intensified feelings, tone, and attitudes, rather than to our message.

Thought 97

Sometimes it's difficult to not have an automatic reaction to what others say or do. When we pause and reflect before we respond, we may communicate our feelings better with an improved objectivity.

Thought 98

When we are mistreated, hurt, or even abused by others, it may feel justified to mistreat, hurt, or abuse ourselves or others, but it may be harmful.

Thought 99

It may be difficult to ask for help. Sometimes we may feel like we don't want it, shouldn't need it, don't deserve it, or we may be a burden to others. It may be courageous to seek help and others may have the ability, the capacity, and the desire to help us.

Thought 100

Sometimes we may have unrealistic expectations to be perfect in certain ways. It may be comforting to accept our perceived imperfections as naturally perfect.

Thought 101

When we accept that material things may be temporary, we may become more grateful for them, and diminish the disappointment that may come when we no longer have them.

Thought 102

When we accept that loved ones may enter and leave our lives, we may feel peace by being grateful for them when they are present and grateful for them when they are gone.

Thought 103

Our loss may be a chance to discover what we have gained.

Thought 104

Our feelings may be valid, but sometimes the thoughts that are correlated with our feelings may be distorted or inaccurate.

Thought 105

When we feel lonely when we are apart from others, cultivating being alone without a feeling of loneliness may let us rely on ourselves more.

Thought 106

When we feel lonely in the company of others, cultivating authentic connections with others may provide us with a sense of belonging.

Thought 107

Authentic connections with others may begin with a genuine interest and curiosity about another.

Thought 108

Our distressing feelings may sometimes be a motivator and a barrier.

Thought 109

Growth within a relationship may be more possible when we understand and accept the place from where our partner may need to begin their progress.

Thought 110

Sometimes we may be unaware that some of our thoughts, feelings, perceptions, and behaviors are no longer as useful as they may have been in the past.

Thought 111

When we learn to fulfill our needs ourselves, we may decrease our dependence on others. This may create more fulfilling relationships.

Thought 112

If we never get the chance to be with someone ever again, it may give us a sense of peace to express all our thoughts and feelings to that person that we would want to convey, without any expectations beyond our own intent to just communicate how we think and feel.

Thought 113

No matter how much we may want to change, help, or influence others, they may stay the same until they want to change.

Thought 114

Well intentioned manipulation of others may elicit desired outcomes for them, but may also leave them without a sense of accomplishment and empowerment.

Thought 115

Uncomfortable or aberrant thoughts, feelings, and behaviors may sometimes be desired in order for us to feel congruent with a distorted perception of ourselves.

Thought 116

It may be more difficult to love when we have a fear.

Thought 117

Regrets may be partly due to our own difficulty forgiving ourselves for doing the best we could, in the capacity we had at the time.

Thought 118

Aberrant thought may sometimes be natural, but may feel wrong or unacceptable. When we don't judge ourselves or others for having these thoughts, we may understand the thoughts better and learn not to invest in, or act upon them.

Thought 119

Sometimes we may need to perceive things as good enough, instead of seeking perfection.

Thought 120

Success may be best appreciated one small accomplishment at a time.

Thought 121

Accepting the discomfort of uncertainty may be comforting.

Thought 122

Because ways of navigating life may be ingrained in us from others, we may not realize that some of these ways may not be useful to ourselves or others.

Thought 123

We may be unaware that we are hurting others because we may have learned from others that it is appropriate.

Thought 124

If beauty is in the eye of the beholder, when we understand others' perspectives, we may see the beauty that others see.

Thought 125

We all may have the ability and the capacity to redeem ourselves.

Thought 126

Some of our difficulties may never truly go away. However, we may be able to get better at mitigating them each time they arise.

Thought 127

We may make inaccurate assumptions about others because we may lack the insight into the difficulties that they face.

Thought 128

If we are in a distressing state, it may be better to diminish the feeling within the state, rather than think about the content of the state, which may exacerbate the feeling.

Thought 129

When we believe our fearful scenarios to be true, we may create distorted perceptions and distressing feelings within ourselves.

Thought 130

Sometimes we may believe that we can control our feelings by thinking of solutions, rather than letting the feelings shift naturally, or creating a shift in ways other than thinking.

Thought 131

Paying attention to our senses may be a way to increase our awareness of our experience.

Thought 132

Observing our thoughts and experiencing our feelings, rather than investing in them, may diminish dissonance and distress.

Thought 133

The more we may attempt to control distressing feelings, the stronger the feelings may become and the longer they may last.

Thought 134

Distortions in our perception may be imperceptible to us because we may naturally believe they are true.

Thought 135

In order to discover how our current perceptions affect ourselves and others, we may need to understand how our past experiences may have shaped our perceptions.

Thought 136

Our past experiences may greatly alter the way we perceive ourselves, others, and our environment, and our perceptions may or may not be accurate.

Thought 137

Sometimes we may believe we need to be prepared for a moment, instead of trusting ourselves in the spontaneity and uncertainty of the moment.

Thought 138

When we consistently cultivate and maintain engagement in the thoughts, activities, and work that make us feel good about ourselves, we may increase our fulfillment.

Thought 139

We may find comfort in habits and behaviors that are unhealthy. We may find it difficult to navigate our lives without them. When these habits are incongruent with ourselves, we may experience dissonance.

Thought 140

Rumination may feel like we are processing or solving a problem, but we may just be exacerbating distressing feelings.

Thought 141

When we incorporate an opposing perspective into our understanding, rather than perpetuate our own perspective, it may increase the understanding of ourselves and others.

Thought 142

We may cultivate connections and understanding when we are respectful of others, even of those whom we don't respect.

Thought 143

When we are honest with our feelings, even when it is difficult, we may cultivate others' understanding of our perspective.

Thought 144

When we have a curiosity and willingness to understand before we act on a desire to explain, we may create more effective communication.

Thought 145

We may become distressed when we base our own fulfillment on others' definition of what is meaningful.

Thought 146

When we are unaware of what is truly fulfilling or meaningful to us, it may become clearer when we cultivate that which inspires us.

Thought 147

When we plan for the future rather than worry about it, the present may be more enjoyable.

Thought 148

When we accept our past rather than think about how it could have been different, we may diminish our feelings of regret.

Thought 149

When we distinguish what is in our control and what is not, it may help us understand what we truly have an effect on.

Thought 150

Sometimes we may involve others in the struggles that are meant for ourselves.

Thought 151

It may be easier to be honest in times of joy, but it may be just as important to be honest during times of sorrow, distress, and conflict.

Thought 152

To increase our understanding of what we may be perceiving, we may need to incorporate others' unique individual perceptions.

Thought 153

Being resilient may mean having a willingness to fail and the strength to try again.

Thought 154

Communication may be more effective when we are expressing feelings without being in a reactive emotional state.

Thought 155

Even good change may be difficult, strange, awkward, uncomfortable, and feel incongruent.

Thought 156

Patience may be a way to appreciate what we have and not what we want.

Thought 157

To do what is congruent with what is ethical, meaningful, and fulfilling to ourselves may be the hardest things to do.

Thought 158

It may take hard work to create, maintain, or repair a good relationship.

Thought 159

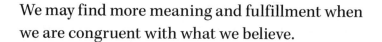

We may find more meaning and fulfillment when
we are congruent with what we believe.

Thought 160

Being vulnerable enough to love may be risky. We may experience immense pain as well as indescribable joy.

Thought 161

Sometimes the way out of an unbearable situation may be to go through it.

Thought 162

We may not realize that we have initial distorted perceptions and interpretations of our experiences, which may alter our perspective and the way we feel about ourselves and others.

Thought 163

When we reflect, we may give ourselves the opportunity to learn about ourselves and others.

Thought 164

Taking time to just experience our experience may be just as productive as doing something.

Thought 165

Observing our environment may be a way to connect with ourselves and the world we are in.

Thought 166

Accepting our thoughts and feelings, rather than trying to change, avoid, or suppress them may allow us to let them arise and subside.

Thought 167

It may be difficult to change what we desire to change about ourselves when we may lack the awareness into why we are the way we are.

Thought 168

Being within nature may give us the opportunity to tune into the natural flow of how we may navigate through our lives.

Thought 169

Experiencing our experience, rather than thinking about it, may create an integration of ourselves within our environment.

Thought 170

To purposefully and knowingly act without thinking about how to act, may create effortless, spontaneous, and more meaningful experiences.

Thought 171

When we cultivate thoughts, feelings, and perceptions that are congruent with ourselves, we may attain more meaning, fulfillment, inspiration, and hope in our lives.

Thought 172

Life may only consist of the meaning we attribute to it.

Love may be like water.

It may be the essence of life. Like the dew, the rain, the river, and the ocean, it may be a system of flow with no absolute source or destination. There may be only a willingness to live within the flow of love.

Index

Printed in the United States
by Baker & Taylor Publisher Services